KU-659-187

a harmony of
ANGELS

"If we saw an angel clearly we should die of pleasure."
Bridget of Sweden, mystic and visionary

a harmony of
ANGELS

Angela McGerr

Illustrations by Richard Rockwood

Quadrille

This book is for all Seekers of the Way of Love and Light, through *hope, courage, truth, beauty, wisdom, harmony* and *healing*.

AUTHOR'S ACKNOWLEDGEMENTS
I should like to dedicate this book to the following people:

🪶 My husband Barry and children, Fleur and Guy, who have had to cope with my sudden and total metamorphosis from businesswoman into healer and angelologist.

🪶 My sister Joanna who first introduced, and then persuaded me on to the rainbow path of healing and angels.

🪶 My sister Fiona who, even before this, talked of her own spiritual inspiration with garden design.

🪶 Renya James who helped to open the first doorway to Love and Light.

🪶 My publishers, and in particular Anne Furniss, who believed in me, and gave invaluable support by encouraging and facilitating the progress of this book.

🪶 My illustrator Richard Rockwood who allowed the angels to assist with the creation of his wonderful illustrations.

🪶 Most of all, however, I thank the angels and ascended masters who guided every step of this project, which has resulted from my own spiritual journey towards enlightenment. Not only did they direct my research with much synchronicity so that I was always able to find the next piece of the jigsaw, but through meditation they provided a great deal of inspiration for the book's contents.

🪶 I am particularly grateful to Seraphiel, Ezekiel, and Cassiel who helped so much in the beginning and Raphael, Haniel, Michael and Melchisadec who are supporting me now with new and ever-more-fascinating projects.

First published in 2001 by Quadrille Publishing Limited
Alhambra House, 27-31 Charing Cross Road, London WC2H OLS

Reprinted in 2001, 2002 (twice)
10 9 8 7 6 5 4

This paperback edition first published in 2003
Reprinted in 2004, 2005, 2006
10 9 8 7 6 5 4

© Text Angela McGerr 2001
© Illustrations Richard Rockwood 2001
© Layout and design Quadrille Publishing Limited 2001
All rights reserved.

British Library Cataloguing in Publication Data
A catalogue record for this book is available from the British Library

ISBN-13: 978 184400 033 3
ISBN-10: 1 84400 033 8

Printed and bound in China

Publishing Director Anne Furniss
Creative Director Mary Evans
Design Jim Smith
Copy Editor Sarah Widdicombe
Editorial Assistant Katie Ginn
Production Sarah Tucker, Vincent Smith

Contents

Introducing angels

"Every visible thing in this world is put under the charge of an angel."
St Augustine

Why this book? Because angels have changed my life in many wonderful ways, and I believe they can change yours - if you let them!

The book is intended for three types of reader. Firstly, it is for those amongst you who are fascinated with the concept of angels in general and would like to know as much as possible about them. It is also hoped that there is new material in this book for enthusiasts to ponder and absorb. Secondly, there are many people who are seeking help, comfort and guidance in their lives to combat stress or overcome difficult situations. Perhaps this could be you, and at this very moment you feel low, as if the world is against you. This book contains self-help information as well as tips and practical exercises, visualisations, rituals and meditations. These are intended to assist you with self-healing, to achieve harmony and tranquillity in your life.

Thirdly, you may be seeking values in life other than materialism and greed. In short, you would like spiritual direction but are not quite sure how to find it, being not entirely comfortable with the organisation and structure of the established churches. The good news is that in learning how to commune with angels (God's messengers) you will never be alone or lack spiritual guidance, for you can call upon angels at any time and in any place and receive their unconditional love.

The information you will find in this book on angels does not come, as you might expect, from the Christian Bible, which names only three angels: Michael, Gabriel and Raphael. Although these are important angels, most of our knowledge comes from other ancient texts, and it is interesting to note that angels transcend any one religion and are found today in Persian, Christian, Jewish and Moslem scriptures. The word 'angel' comes from the Greek *angelos* meaning messenger, and, surprising as it may seem, although we can always call on our guardian angel there are also hundreds of named angels for given situations, from whom we can choose to ask for specific help.

In the past, people believed and trusted in calling on angelic help. This faith was then lost, but is now being rediscovered. One of the sources of this belief was Essene Angelology. Around two thousand years ago a religious sect named the Essenes lived in Qumran, on the shores of the Dead Sea. Some sources state that Jesus Christ was an Essene. Certainly the Essenes were skilled at healing and practised angelology. They believed that it was necessary to harmonise oneself physically and spiritually to achieve wellbeing, and that the way to do this was to commune with angels daily. They are thought to have written most, if not all, of the Dead Sea Scrolls, and the angels in this book are taken from these and other ancient documents.

What are angels exactly? This book does not concern itself with fallen angels, or demons, for obvious reasons. To be able to call upon angels for daily and loving assistance, I have included only those who have been variously described as the Shining Ones, Light Beings, or the Breath of God (*Spiritus Dei*).

The consensus is that, unlike spirit guides, who have once been human and chosen to return and help the living, angels have, in the main, never been human. (There are a few exceptions to this: some biblical characters, such as St Francis of Assisi, are said to have become angels upon death). Interestingly, sometimes the reverse is also true, Archangel Michael was sanctified by the Christian church and became St Michael.

Angels, then, are beings of pure spirit who dwell in the ether, which is the fifth element (the others are earth, air, fire, and water). Are they male or female? We don't really know – there are some and some. They may be androgynous, or you can simply decide for yourself. They are always there around us, although they cannot intercede unless we specifically ask them to help us – hence this book.

The book is designed to open a door for you into the loving world of angels. It is your decision whether you walk through this door or walk past. Invoke Tabris, Angel of Free Will, to guide you to make the right choice for yourself. If, as I did, you decide to invite angels into your life, start from today. Read on, learn, trust, and you will start to benefit from the Way of Love and Light, the most powerful forces in the Universe.

Invoking angels

Angels will help you anywhere and at any time – all you need to do is ask, with love and trust in your heart. Whether your need is to find a loving relationship, to gain abundance and success in your life, to clarify your hopes and dreams for the future, to find strength, courage or empowerment to fight your battles, or to find self-healing, inner peace and serenity, angels can give you loving assistance.

TRUST AND INTENT. It is important to remember that the true purpose of calling on angels in daily life is to support your own efforts. They are not there to help you win the lottery. Beware, also, of calling on angels if your cause is not just. They will come to your aid only if:

You are asking from your heart with sincerity and love
You trust and believe in the result
Your intentions and reasons for asking for help are honourable

THE POWER OF THE NAMES AND THE NUMBER THREE. Throughout this book, and in the Appendix of Angels (page 94) you will find a host (or harmony) of angels who can help you with specific life situations. The names themselves, which are thousands of years old, contain powerful energy when spoken out loud, and this power is increased when they are voiced three times in accordance with the Universal Law of Three.

When invoking angels, wherever possible respect the Law of Three, an esoteric concept that has been handed down from ancient times. Two of the best known examples of it are the Holy Trinity and man's components: mind, body and spirit.

A SIMPLE INVOCATION. Choose an angel to help you with your own special need and call the angel by name three times. Then ask this angel to be with you, completing your invocation by saying the words 'In Love and Light' three times, to show your intent is honest. For instance, you might say:

Raphael, Raphael, Raphael (or other chosen angel name)
Please be with me now (or other request)
In Love and Light, in Love and Light, in Love and Light.

A DEEPER FOCUS ON ANGELS. Sometimes a short meditation, perhaps with some relaxing music, can be very effective; six suggested meditations are included in the book. On page 17 we suggest you create your own home sanctuary or sacred space in which to commune with your angels.

If your life is so rushed that you don't have time to do a meditation, sit down quietly and take some deep, calming breaths. Try to take your focus within and imagine that when you are breathing in, you are breathing in white light, and when you breathe out you are ridding yourself of harmful emotions. When you have breathed out all the things you want to release, continue breathing in and out white light, so that you become surrounded with white. Invoke your angelic helper while in this peaceful frame of mind.

A WORD OF THANKS. Always remember to thank your angels for responding to your call. They have given you unconditional love, so send them your love in return. If you open your heart you will soon sense them around you; acknowledge their presence and thank them for their assistance.

DECIDING WHICH ANGEL TO APPROACH. As you now know, you can ask for angelic support by using the method of invocation described above. But how will you know which angel to invoke for a particular situation in your life?

As a starting point, there are seven Angel Rulers, one for each day of the week. Each of these powerful beings, apart from governing a specific day, has control over a different life situation, as well as having a planetary and crystal connection. Each chapter, therefore, majors on a different Angel Ruler from Monday through to Sunday. The first chapter is about Gabriel, ruler of Monday, the Moon and moonstones. He is the angel for dreams, hopes and aspirations in life, so if this is the area in which you need help, you can invoke Gabriel, particularly on a Monday, perhaps wearing a moonstone to bring him closer to you. Similarly, Camael, Angel Ruler of Tuesday, rules Mars and is the angel for ruby or garnet. He helps us with justifiable anger, energy and empowerment in battling for what we know to be right.

Within each chapter we also explore related problems and issues, listing a variety of other angels who can assist in these circumstances. By reading and absorbing each chapter you will find a key to improving your inner harmony within the whole spectrum of life's challenges.

Finally, for quick reference purposes, the A-Z of Angels on page 94 details 100 angels and their special areas of influence. Remember they are always there to help you.

In Love and Light; In Love and Light; In Love and Light.

Gabriel: *hopes, dreams & aspirations*

Gabriel, whose name means 'God is my Strength', is known as the 'Heavenly Awakener'. He is the angel who reveals the meaning of our dreams and supports our aspirations in life. Above all, he brings us the gift of hope. Ruler of the moon and the first heaven (see page 24), Gabriel dictated the Koran to Mohammed and is said to have inspired Joan of Arc. To the Moslems, Gabriel (known as Jibral) is the spirit of truth; to the Jews, he was adviser to Joseph and the Children of Israel; to the Christians he revealed to Mary that she would conceive and bear the baby Jesus.

We all have dreams and aspirations – Gabriel can help us to focus on these and clarify what we really want from life and why we want it. Consider your personal ambition – if it is to make money, are you really sure that this will make you happy? Perhaps you really want what money can buy, as a way of proving your worth to others? But in reality this may be because you are uncomfortable with your current path through life. Is it time you reviewed your prospects?

Are you focused, or are you drifting, lacking purpose and having difficulty in relating to friends and colleagues? How many times have you found yourself arriving somewhere, even by car, without the faintest idea how you got there? This is all well and good if you are just exceptionally busy (and we all suffer from it to some extent) but, if it happens all the time, you may be trying to escape from an unhappy situation. If this is the case, Gabriel can help you to ground yourself, face reality and then reappraise your hopes and dreams. Don't wait until it's too late.

As ruler of Monday and the moon, Gabriel can help to draw in the power of the moon, which is feminine or right-brained energy, allowing you to develop your intuitive ability. This, combined with your left-brained logic and analytical skills, will lead to balance and help you to understand and realise your true potential. Although you can ask for Gabriel's support at any time, Monday is a particularly good day for seeking his wise counsel.

Finding the name of your guardian angel

"I am the Angel of the Moon, darkened to be rekindled soon beneath the azure cope.
Nearest to earth, it is my ray that best illumines the midnight way,
I bring the gift of Hope."
The Golden Legend – Gabriel, Henry Wadsworth Longfellow

We all have a guardian angel who is with us to offer loving support from birth until death. Your guardian angel is there to help you to ground and focus in order to realise your goals in life, and you probably feel that you would like to address this angel by name. There are several ways of finding out the name – you could ask to be told in a dream (see page 36), or in meditation (see page 18). Another way is simply to invoke your guardian angel and ask for the name to be given to you. What then happens is that you will receive a name mentally; it may well be just an everyday name – by no means all angels have complicated or Hebrew-sounding names.

If the name you have received is correct, you will come across it again more than once, by means of angel synchronicity. One way of checking is to ask for the name again and then switch on the radio to a music station – you may well find the name in a song that then plays. It is also possible that you might buy or borrow a book, or watch a film or play on television, and strangely, the same name will appear. There is no such thing as coincidence when you are around angels – all these things will be meant to happen so that you know you are on the right path.

🪶 AN ANGEL STORY. A lady named Jo attended one of my Rainbow Angel Workshops recently and said that when asking for her guardian angel's name she received the name Eric. "Surely this can't be right," she commented. I explained that if it were correct she would quickly receive further confirmation. A week later she wrote to tell me what had happened after the workshop. Driving to a friend's house the following day she saw a beautiful rainbow. Next, in the kitchen she noticed a fridge magnet with the word Eric printed on it. Subsequently, at a cousin's house, she came across a bean-filled toy. On asking about it she was told it was called 'Flat Eric'. Then they went into the garden and found several white feathers. On their way home her mother had bought a couple of houseplants and when she took off the wrapping paper, what should be inside but a tiny bronze angel. "Well," she said, "It must have fallen in there by mistake as there were so many Christmas decorations around". Jo was finally convinced that these messages proved that Eric was the name of her guardian angel.

Five ways of knowing an angel is with you

"Love, then, is the most intelligent and creative force in the universe. It is literally the vine that ties and supports all life and creation together." Flower of Life 2000 Workbook

Angels give you pure, unconditional love. Here are some typical methods they may use to send you messages, or to respond to your invocations by indicating their presence in your life.

🪶 FINDING A TINY WHITE FEATHER. This indicates that you are on the right path. A door has opened for you in your life, and you have chosen to walk through. In accordance with the Universal Law of Three, you may well find two more.

🪶 A SUDDEN FRAGRANCE UNDER YOUR NOSE. If you suddenly smell a fragrance which seems to come and go, and it's nothing to do with your own perfume or body spray, or your surroundings, it's likely to be your guardian angel signifying approval for what you are doing. You'll probably continue to smell the same fragrance from time to time, perhaps when you are talking to your angel or in the same part of your house.

🪶 A BRIGHT LIGHT OR COLOUR WITHIN YOUR MIND. You've closed your eyes and asked for angelic help. You receive a sudden flash of illumination within your mind. It may momentarily fill your mind with light, or may pass across your inner vision like a shooting star. It can also be a pulsing shape or colour (often gold or purple). All these manifestations mean your plea has been heard.

🪶 TINGLING IN THE AIR. Hold your hand out in front of you or above your head after a short meditation in which you have asked angels for their support. You will feel a tingling against your hand, like a gentle electric current – angels are around you. If you then call in another angel, the tingling will increase or change in nature. If at first you don't feel anything keep trying, and after a while you will begin to sense the energy. You may also see tiny points of light in your peripheral vision.

🪶 A FEELING OF LOVING WARMTH. Often when you have invoked an angel with a feeling of love and trust, in response you will feel filled with warmth, comfort or peace. This is particularly noticeable as heat in the palms of your hands or around your heart. It may be a wave of love pouring right through you before ebbing away.

Creating a home sanctuary or sacred space

Find a suitable room or corner in your home, where from time to time you will be able to be undisturbed. Use your sanctuary as a sacred space for meditation, rituals, contemplation or just quiet relaxation and re-charging of your spirit. If you can't keep them permanently on display, keep all the items listed below in your treasure box (see page 29) or on a shelf until you need them. The basic ingredients for your sacred space are to draw you closer to angels in general and therefore focus on white. For other rituals in this book we suggest colours, crystals and oils specific to those rituals.

You will need:

A circular or square piece of silver, gold or white cloth (or a cushion if preferred); a white feather (or feather-trimmed cushion); a clear quartz crystal; a white candle; a small bowl of spring water or indoor water feature

Optional extras

An oil burner, for which you select either a general cleansing fragrance such as sage or frankincense or one specific to your needs, (see also page 90); a small mirror on which to stand your crystal; blossoms or tumblestones to place in the spring water bowl

- Check the north/south/east/west orientation.
- Place the cloth or cushion in the centre of your chosen site.
- Place the feather in the north, representing angels and air.
- Place the crystal in the west to represent the earth. Put it on a mirror to enhance the effect and energy. (For cleansing crystals see page 29).
- Place the candle in the east for the fire element.
- The bowl of spring water, or water feature, goes in the south.
- If you are using an oil burner, sage or frankincense will cleanse the air of negativity before a meditation or ritual.
- Ask your guardian angel to fill your sacred space with love and light, and to help you guard and preserve it always.

A meditation with Gabriel to draw down the power of the moon

"… and pluck till time and times are done, the silver apples of the moon, the golden apples of the sun" W.B. Yeats

This evening meditation will help you to gain a new perspective in regard to your life, so that you can re-define your pathway. If you feel the need to expand your creative energy to new challenges, do this meditation in the first quarter after the new moon. Choose the full moon, however, for drawing in energy to complete a major project or finalise a situation so that you can start afresh. Whichever moon phase you choose, view the moon and feel the mystery of her clear, silver light. The energy of the moon is feminine while that of the sun is masculine. Use the energies of your own home sanctuary to help with this meditation, using a silver candle and moonstone instead of the quartz and white candle.

- Ask angels to surround you completely with protective white or golden light during this meditation. In your mind see the radiance all around you.
- Imagine roots growing from your feet into the floor, anchoring and grounding.
- Take some slow, deep breaths in and out and try to focus on your inner self.
- Feel yourself relaxing. Let external sounds fade away and maintain your focus within. Count to yourself – 1: relaxing; 2: going deeper; 3: becoming calm.
- Imagine a vertical column or meridian line within your body, extending downwards from the crown of your head, through your brow, throat, heart, solar plexus, stomach, to the base of your spine.
- Visualise the moon and imagine her pure light. Draw this silver radiance down into your crown, which is your spiritual connection to the cosmos. Next feel the energy filling your brow, reaching your intuition, subconscious and the world of your dreams. Now it travels down to your throat.
- Now imagine the energy flowing down the meridian line to your heart, and then send it out and down from there to fill every cell in your body.
- Invoke Gabriel and then ask him to help you focus the powerful energy of the moon to your heart and your mind, to help you understand and develop your own true potential.
- Feel yourself filled with purpose and a renewed sense of direction. Enjoy.
- Count from 3 to 1 to return to full awareness, ensuring you feel grounded, open your eyes when ready. Thank the angels for their loving assistance.

Angels and crystal energy

🌙 MAIN ANGEL INFLUENCERS. For each of these chapters there is an angel who can be a main influence in your life. When calling on these angels, you can also increase the power of your meditations and self-development exercises by using crystal energy; this will raise your vibrational level so it is closer to that of the ether, the angelic realm. Hold the relevant crystal in the left hand (always use your left hand to receive cosmic energy and your right hand to give energy back to the Universe).

There are crystal associations for each of the angels governing the chapters, that can be summarised and linked to key issues as follows:

Gabriel	Moonstone, selenite	Hopes, dreams, aspirations
Camael	Ruby, garnet, red agate, carnelian	Courage, empowerment, justice
Michael	Sapphire, blue (or yellow) topaz	Strength, protection, truth
Zadkiel	Lapis lazuli, turquoise	Abundance, wisdom, success
Haniel	Rose quartz, emerald, tourmaline	Love, compassion, beauty
Cassiel	Obsidian, black-and-white agate, jet	Peace, harmony, serenity
Raphael	Clear quartz, diamond	Healing, energy, knowledge

There are also crystals for the elemental healing angels: Phul (aquamarine), Uriel (amber) and Ariel (amethyst), (see the Cassiel meditation on page 80).

🌙 SPECIAL ANGELIC CRYSTALS. There are three special crystals which are also used for contacting the angelic realm. They are celestite, angelite and selenite.

Celestite itself means 'of the sky', and when compressed it is a pale sky blue in colour. In this form it is known as angelite, and the white banding can look like wings. When not compressed, celestite can be different colours of white through yellow to brown. Its general properties are to aid contact with angels and, having done so, to receive communication through clairaudience (receiving a message in your head) or dreams.

Selenite is a beautiful translucent white crystal that, when polished, can shine like moonlight itself. It is a calm, serene and pure stone, helping the user to clarify thought and develop inner consciousness. It can also be used for past life recall and psychic protection. Selenite is particularly helpful when invoking Gabriel for assistance, as an alternative to moonstone.

Rutilated quartz is another crystal which has an angelic significance. It is clear quartz crystal which has inclusions of fine needles of rutile. These often look like angel hair which has been trapped within the crystal, making it appropriate for using with angel meditations and giving rise to its nickname.

A large crystal may have an opening leading to its heart (sometimes called a gateway); this connects more deeply with the angelic realm.

🦅 DOWSING WITH A CRYSTAL. With a little practice, dowsing can be an effective way of obtaining help and guidance from your guardian or other angels. Do not be afraid to try it. For preference, dowse with a clear crystal pendulum held on a fine cord. Before starting, cleanse the object (see page 29).

🦅 Wind the cord around your third finger, taking it across your middle finger and suspending it from the index finger. Leave about 15cm/6in of cord between your finger and the pendulum itself.

🦅 Close your eyes and ask for your guardian angel, and Michael, to be with you and to surround you completely with protective golden light and truth.

🦅 Next, ask a question to which you know the answer, so that you can test the pendulum's response to 'yes' and 'no'. For example: "Is my name (your name)?" The most frequent response will be for the pendulum to swing clockwise in a circle for 'yes' and in a straight line for 'no'. When you have established your responses, ask the pendulum 3 times to confirm that the answers you will receive are in Divine Truth.

🦅 If there is no clear answer to your question, or if you have framed it so that there is more than one answer, the pendulum will not move but will tremble.

🦅 If you need to make a choice between, say, four different possibilities, write them down clearly on a piece of paper divided into four sections. Then dowse over each in turn for your answer.

🦅 If you have a question for Gabriel regarding your hopes and dreams, ask it through your pendulum. You will probably be surprised at how much help you receive. It does get easier with practice. Remember to thank those angels who assisted.

Camael: *courage, empowerment & justice*

Camael, whose name means 'He Who Sees God', represents courage with nobility and has sometimes been depicted in the guise of a leopard crouched on a rock. Camael has been described by ancient sources as 'a name which personifies divine justice'. He has always been associated with Mars, the red planet and god of war; his day is Tuesday. He is ruler of powers and fifth heaven. Camael, then, stands for the righting of wrongs, or comfort and support in situations of justifiable anger. Have you felt yourself to be the victim of a miscarriage of justice? Even if it is relatively minor, the sense of indignation is strong and may never be entirely lost, leading to internalisation of anger or bitterness and blocking of your personal progress. Or it may be that you judge yourself too severely or set impossibly high standards. It is vitally important that you learn forgiveness and acceptance of yourself and others; only then can you take control of your life and move on.

Perhaps right here and now you have a battle looming, in which right is definitely on your side, or perhaps you are fighting for a loved one in a situation where there is a need for fairer treatment – a continuing trial of strength where the outcome is uncertain. If this scenario sounds familiar, invoke Camael to empower you to fight passionately for what you believe in.

Then there is fear. Many of us feel anxious at times, about life, the future, the world in general. This is perfectly understandable in this stressful age, but fear constricts us, creates boundaries and causes a contraction of spirit. This prevents development of our full potential as well as our spiritual growth, while love causes us to expand both these aspects of ourselves. Camael (who is said to have given comfort and solace to Jesus in the Garden of Gethsemane) can guide you in what is known as 'the dark and lonely night of the soul'. You can ask Camael for strength to enable you to confront your fears and, having done so, for the courage, energy and determination to overcome them.

Camael's crystals are ruby, garnet, red agate, and also bloodstone or red carnelian. Red crystals are for strength, energy, passion and courage; bloodstone (believed to be the blood of Jesus falling on green jasper) assists with fighting injustice.

The angelic realms where angels dwell

There are said to be seven heavens, the seventh of which is the abode of God, hence the saying about happiness: 'being in seventh heaven'. According to ancient sources, the angels of the presence (of God the Creator), are rulers of each of the heavens: Gabriel (first heaven), Camael (fifth), Michael (fourth), Zadkiel (sixth), Raphael (second), Haniel (third) and Cassiel (gatekeeper for the seventh heaven and the Creator). This is why we have chosen one of each of these powerful angels to watch over each chapter of this book.

What about hell? All beings have free will, even angels, who were allowed one choice for all time, between darkness and light. Those who chose darkness followed Satan and became demons or fallen angels. Some writings stated that hell was located in second or third heaven, however, it was later felt that this was confusing to dead souls, so hell was banished to its own region 'down below'. All angels who chose light are believed to reside in orders within the three angelic spheres (or hierarchies) according to their rank. Although the exact order within the hierarchies varies according to the source, they are generally accepted to be as follows:

The first sphere of three: seraphim, cherubim, thrones, rulers Raphael, Michael and Cassiel; the most senior angels – nearest to God and heavenly counsellors, with responsibility for the music of the spheres, the movement of the heavens, the stars, and guardians of the planets.

The second sphere of three: dominions, powers, virtues, rulers Zadkiel, Camael and Haniel; middle-ranking angels – heavenly governors, responsible for the integration of the spiritual and material worlds, for beaming out divine energy for healing and for bearing the conscience of humanity, including religions and world history.

The third sphere of three: angel princes (or principalities), archangels, angels, rulers Haniel, Gabriel and Raphael. Angels who function as heavenly messengers, and those closest to man, being guardian angels of nations, cities, corporations/businesses, and providing guardian and companion angels to mankind.

Creating a treasure box

🖊 This book suggests many ways to help you live your future life in a slightly different way, using ancient energies and knowledge. It may be that from now onwards you will look on things with a new eye, perhaps as a result of the tiny white feathers you find, or the crystals and candles you use.

If you try out the rituals contained within the chapters, you will also need to create or obtain the different-coloured circular and square cloths (or perhaps cushions) on which to place the various crystals and candles. You may also have made or purchased a pendulum for dowsing (see page 21). Why not create a treasure box in which to keep your candles, crystals and other meditation aids. Keep the box in your own sacred place or home sanctuary (see page 17).

Start with the box itself, and try to ensure it is made of natural materials. Either make one by covering cardboard with natural fabric or paper, or look out for an attractive wooden box at craft or antique fairs. In the box you can keep all your treasures. Your pendulum can be placed in a small pouch or wrapped in a scrap of silk (choose a chakra colour or colours that you feel to be appropriate). If you have any angel cards to store, these should also be wrapped in silk.

Before using the pendulum or crystals, cleanse them three times in clear, cold running water or in the sun's rays (for as long as you can), before replacing them in your treasure box. You can also energise them by placing them for one night in the light of the full moon.

Alternatively, ask the angels of the elements to help you to cleanse and energise your treasures, by invoking each in turn and imagining the items being cleansed. Therefore, invoke Phul, Lord of the Waters, and visualise in your mind the items being washed clean in a clear stream or pool. Alternatively, invoke Uriel, Angel of Fire, and imagine the items in the heart of a candle flame, or invoke Ariel, Angel of Earth and Air, and see blue-purple earth energy flowing around and through them.

🖊 ANGEL FEATHERS. So many people have telephoned me and spoken of finding a white feather that I have lost count of the number. I, myself, found my first white feather on the day I learned about healing, long before I began my angel research. One led to more, and now here I am, the author of this book. When you start to find your own tiny white feathers (and you will) place them in your sacred space or home sanctuary or glue them around a small mirror – that way you will be viewing yourself surrounded by protective angel feathers.

Putting your life in divine order

"Even as the stone of the fruit must break, that its heart may stand in the sun, so must you know pain."
The Prophet, Khalil Gibran

❧ MANAGING ANGER AND BITTERNESS. Angels can help you when you have said entirely the wrong thing and been tactless and hurtful. Perhaps you were justifiably angry and in the heat of the moment you made an unfortunate remark, which could not then be unsaid. You immediately regretted your outburst, but at the time your pride prevented you from apologising. These quarrels, if left, become harder and harder to retrieve – some families spend years not speaking to each other over such incidents. Perhaps you have just such a situation in your life which angels can help to overcome.

❧ EMPOWERMENT THROUGH FORGIVENESS. First of all, you may need to forgive yourself for something you have done so that you can heal the past. This is not easy, but Camael can help you empower yourself to come to terms with your actions and, through self-acceptance of your faults, to move on in your life. Try the meditation on page 26.

If you owe apologies to others, the angel Phanuel is the one to help you to handle the situation and make amends in the best possible way. Don't let the sadness or bitterness go on any longer, as you are surrounding yourself with negative energy. Ask Michael to help you with the right words, or Adnachiel, Angel of Sagittarius, if you tend to be too blunt. If the other person refuses to accept your atonement, you will still have dispelled negativity from yourself. If someone wants to apologise to you, give them time and space. It does take guts either to apologise gracefully or to receive apologies with dignity, but whichever way round it is, such effort is never wasted.

If you need self-confidence in order to be able to take any of these steps, ask Haniel or Machidiel, Angel of Aries, to assist.

❧ STRESSES AND STRAINS WITH FRIENDS AND FAMILY. In all relationships there is stress in day-to-day life, particularly when living in close proximity to others. At such times make space for yourself, and if you lack inner harmony seek assistance from Cassiel (see Chapter 6). Remember that you can invoke the following angels: Achaiah: Angel of Patience, is sure to be needed from time to time. Ambriel, Angel of Gemini, is a problem-solving angel, while Melchisadec, Prince of Peace, is sometimes equated with the Holy Spirit; in times of serious trouble he can be invoked to help bring peace, healing and tranquillity to your household.

🪶 CHANGING YOUR LIFE FOR THE BETTER. If you are unhappy, take the time to consider your real needs and wants, and then determine how you can make changes within yourself in order to start to satisfy these needs. Be honest with yourself and then make the necessary decisions.

Try the ritual with Ascended Master St Germain and the Violet Flame Angels on page 33. This ritual is to enable your spiritual transmutation, to change/transmute old energy and thought patterns and thereby allow new attitudes to develop within you.

🪶 SAYING A PRAYER WITH SANDALPHON. Many people feel comforted or strengthened by prayer at times of great trial. If you feel this way, an angel of particular help is Sandalphon. He is the angel who collects prayers and conveys them to God on your behalf. In the words of Longfellow's poem *Sandalphon*, it was said of him, rather beautifully:

"And he gathers the prayers as he stands,
And they change into flowers in his hands
Into garlands of purple and red;
And beneath the great arch of the portal,
Through the streets of the City Immortal
Is wafted the fragrance they shed."

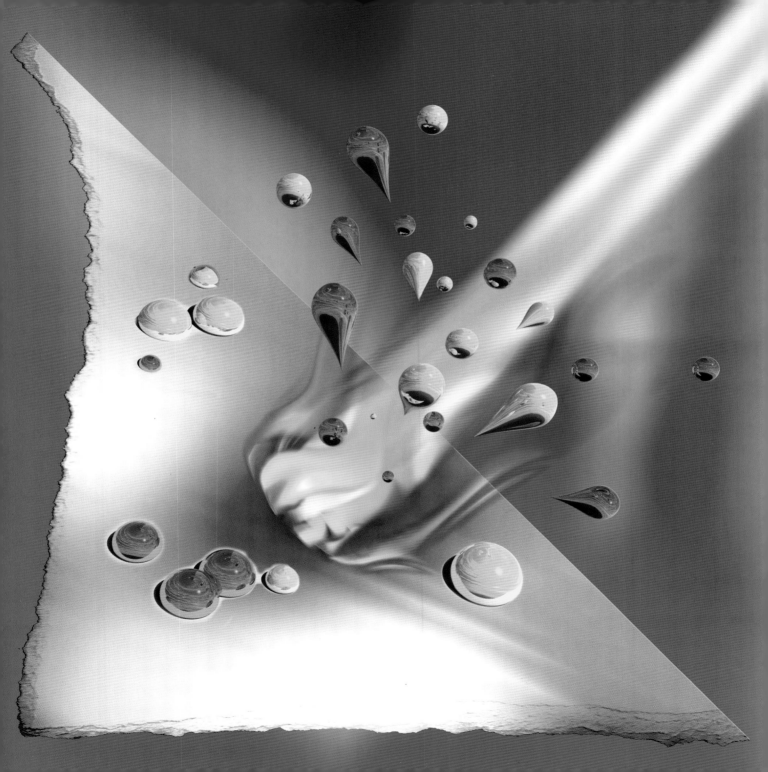

Self-transformation with spiritual alchemy

You can bring a little spiritual alchemy to yourself by means of this ritual by using it to rid yourself of old, negative behavioural patterns. Ascended Master St Germain (see page 90) is the Guardian of the Silver Violet Fire, assisted by the Violet Flame Angels. When any dark, negative energy from within you is sent to this fire it is immediately converted back to white light, or positive energy, leaving you free to re-programme yourself for the future.

You will need:
A violet altar cloth or cushion, a piece of amethyst and a violet candle (for St Germain); lavender oil; a CD of meditative music (optional)

- Set up your ritual with the violet cloth and amethyst crystal.
- Now anoint the violet candle with a drop of lavender oil and light it.
- Write down on a piece of paper those behavioural habits or thought patterns you wish to transform.
- Invoke St Germain and the Violet Flame Angels, ask to be surrounded completely with silver violet fire, and speak the following incantation:

"In the name of the Seventh Ray, I call forth St Germain, the Violet Flame Angels and the energies of the silver violet fire. I ask from my heart that this energy flows through me, through each of the chakras, unblocking old energy patterns, purifying body, mind and soul and allowing new growth to take place, in Love and Light, Love and Light, Love and Light. As I release from myself these blockages, may they be transmuted into the white light of Divine Goodness. I am the silver violet fire, I am the purity God desires."

- As you say the final sentence, visualise the silver violet fire entering your crown chakra, travelling down, cleansing and purifying each chakra in turn, and then exiting from your base chakra. Now imagine blue healing rays cauterising any cavities, followed by yellow and green rays starting the process of new growth and development within you.
- Thank St Germain and all the angels for their loving assistance.
- Burn the piece of paper on which you wrote earlier, ensuring it burns down completely to ash. As it does so, mentally draw a line under the image of your old self, ready for the new. Bury the ash in the ground and dwell no more on it.

Michael: *strength, protection & truth*

On Wednesday, we focus on Michael, according to many writings one of the greatest of all angels. His name means 'Who is as God', and apart from being equated with St George, patron saint of England, and St Michael, he appears in Christian, Persian, Moslem and Jewish texts. Ruler of fourth heaven, he is recorded in the Dead Sea Scrolls as the Prince of Light, the chief warrior against darkness.

Michael represents strength in body and spirit, and brings rescue to us in the form of his sword and his cloak of cobalt blue. You can visualise the sword as either metal or living flame; either way, it can cut away the darkness of fear, illness or other negative emotions within us, allowing light, strength and blue healing energy to come in. Michael's blue cloak shields us from harmful energy and invokes protection for ourselves or our loved ones.

Michael is also described as the Logos (the Word); in this context, the Word symbolises truth in all its guises: having the courage to be honest with ourselves and in our dealings with others, and being loyal to our principles when presenting our own truth to the world. In other words, Michael helps us with clarity in communication at all levels. He is an angel to call upon in all sorts of situations, for instance if: you need physical strength to get through the next hour, day or week; you wish to cut the ties that bind, in the case of rejection, in order to be freed from your hurt; a situation needs retrieval: ask Michael for the necessary patience, calmness and dialogue to deal with it; your life is suddenly dark and you are afraid; Michael can cut away the darkness and give you spiritual protection. Having addressed your personal truth, and released unwanted aspects of yourself, you can now start to grow physically and spiritually stronger with the help of Michael, Prince of Light.

The crystals for Michael are sapphire, blue or yellow topaz and citrine. The blue stones are for peacefulness, healing and health, the golden stones help to initiate positive action, improve communication and expand life's possibilities.

Angels and communication

"I fled Him, down the nights and down the days;
I fled Him, down the arches of the Years;
I fled Him, down the labyrinthine ways
Of my own mind; and in the mist of tears
I hid from Him, and under running laughter.
Up vistaed slopes, I sped; and shot precipitated,
Adown Titanic glooms of chasmed fears,
From those strong Feet that followed, followed after."
The Hound of Heaven, Frances Thompson

ANGELIC MESSAGES. Meditation can be very effective, but there are many other ways of communicating with angels. One is to ask your questions out loud and channel the answers in your head; this is a form of clairaudience. To practise this, you need to relax and sit comfortably in your armchair (with pencil and paper) or at your desk. Detach yourself from your surroundings with some deep breaths, and focus your mind within. Ask to be surrounded with light and for Michael or your guardian angel to be with you. Frame your question and an answer will come into your head. Note it down immediately.

You can also send an etheric message with an angelic bow and arrow of gold. To do this, imagine writing your message on a piece of paper, then tying the paper to the golden arrow with a piece of ribbon. Then visualise drawing back the bow and firing off the arrow to the recipient. In your mind see the message being received. Because it is sent etherically it will arrive at the speed of thought, as in the etheric dimension time and space do not exist. With practice, the other person can send you a reply the same way and this method can become amazingly effective.

ANGELS AND DREAMS. Your dreams are expressions of your subconscious mind and can contain specific angelic guidance or messages. When asleep, we no longer have the continuous distractions of daily life. This can also apply during meditation, as when we switch off or de-focus the conscious mind, it enables angels to communicate with us more easily.

If you are worried about something, you could ask for a reply to be given to you in your dreams. The easiest way to do this is to compose a short poem, incorporating your question, then say it over and over to yourself just before you go to sleep. This will place the question in your subconscious. On waking, you may have clearly received the answer; be sure to keep a 'dream diary' next to your bed so you can write it down immediately.

🖊 NEW WAYS WITH WORDS. As well as Michael, there are other angels who can help you to improve your communication skills at home or at work. The angel Achaiah brings patience when your temper is stretched to breaking point. Ambriel is a problem-solving angel for stressful workdays, or to help you to listen to other people's troubles in a positive way (see also Haniel's Pink Mirror, page 69). Sadriel, Angel of Order, can help you to sort out your thoughts or deal calmly with moments of chaos. Eth is the angel who is charged with ensuring that all the meetings and deliverables that you plan occur at the right time, but if you intend to invoke Eth be sure you are ready yourself.

🖊 AN ANGEL STORY.
Those who attend my Rainbow Angel Workshops are always asked why they have chosen the course. One lady, Margaret, related how she had received an angelic communication. Hurrying to leave a supermarket car park, she went to reverse her car out of the parking space. A voice in her head told her to STOP, and without knowing why she stopped immediately. A few seconds later a frantic parent appeared; an unseen toddler had run away from him and was in a blind spot right behind her car. The child would certainly have been injured if she hadn't stopped when she did. Margaret was convinced this was divine intervention, and it had brought her to find out more about angels.

Five ways of invoking protection for loved ones

"Many roads hast thou fashioned and all of them lead to the light."
Hymn to Mithras the Sun God, Rudyard Kipling

You may not realise the power of your mind and will, which is why it is so important that it is linked with love and an honest intent. As you become practised in calling on angels, and in meditation, your ability to visualise angels and concepts will gradually grow, until you will see them clearly in your mind. Practise the following, which are very useful protective visualisations:

🪶 Place yourself, or another, inside a golden egg filled with light, and ask Raphael, Angel of the Sun and Healing, to ensure that this egg does not break.

🪶 To prevent negativity reaching you or a loved one you can protect with an aura of violet, which transmutes negativity before it reaches you. Imagine a pyramid and place yourself or the other person(s) within that pyramid. Then ask St Germain and the Violet Flame Angels to fill the pyramid with violet fire. Next imagine the figure leaving the pyramid but remaining outlined in violet. You can also do this with cars or other means of transportation such as aeroplanes.

🪶 Ask for the help of Michael, in terms of his blue cloak. Ask for the cloak to be wrapped around your loved one to protect them from harm. Visualise the colour of the cloak, which is cobalt blue, and the hood, and then see it enveloping completely from head to foot.

🪶 Ask Haniel to place a rose-pink bubble around someone, and to make it strong and flexible enough to protect them until you ask again.

🪶 For temporary invisibility, ask Gabriel to place a silver cloak around a person or an object, such as your house or car. Again, imagine it completely covering you or the item in question.

Always remember to give sincere thanks to the angels for their loving assistance.

You can do these visualisations as often as you like, and include them in a meditation. On page 84, we suggest a way of sending healing to loved ones with a golden energy ball. If they need healing and protection, send the healing first and then invoke one of the above angelic protections on their behalf.

Angels, rainbows and colours

"You are the colour you choose." Vicky Wall

🖋 THE SIGNIFICANCE OF WHITE. There are angels (and Ascended Masters, see page 91) connected with each colour of the rays of the rainbow, but all angels are linked with white, which is the sum of the seven rainbow colours. White and white feathers are particular symbols of angels for the following reasons:

🖋 White symbolises purity and the way of love and light.
🖋 White is protective.
🖋 White is the unification of the seven colours of the rainbow; the sum is greater than the parts.
🖋 White is the colour of spirituality, depicted as being above the crown chakra.
🖋 The feather represents softness and gentleness combined with strength.
🖋 The feather is a symbol for the element of air linking it with healing, communication and the soul.
🖋 The white feather represents the Dove, symbol of the Holy Spirit and pure, unconditional love.

Once you have found the tiny white feather, which has opened for you this spiritual doorway, always carry it around with you to remind you of your new journey. When you have a collection, use them to form a circle around the altar cloth and candle in your sacred place (see page 17). Crystalline white is associated with the angels Seraphiel and Cassiel (and also Ascended Master Serapis Bey) and may be invoked to help consider all that has happened to you in your life and to put it into appropriate context for the future.

🖋 VIOLET/PURPLE. Violet is the colour of cosmic awareness, and of our link with the Creator. Invoke the angel Ariel, Angel of the elements of Earth and Air, to focus on this colour, or wear it to help develop your spirituality. Violet is also protective, as it rids you of negativity, acting rather like a spiritual antiseptic. See also the ritual for self-transformation on page 33.

Think purple to aid psychic development and expansion of the mind. Invoke Barakiel to develop your psychic sense, but be sure to combine this with spiritual growth, as you can be spiritual but not psychic or psychic without being spiritual.

FOUR REASONS TO THINK BLUE.

Blue is for healing. There are many blue healing colours: sky blue is for communication, blue-purple is for earth energy, cobalt blue is cauterising, powder blue is associated with the healing power of air.

Blue is for relaxation. If you are agitated or cannot get to sleep, visualise yourself surrounded with dark, indigo blue which is calming and brings peace. This is also the colour for celestial wisdom, and is linked with Zadkiel (as is turquoise).

Blue is for protection. Envelop yourself completely in Michael's cobalt-blue cloak whenever you feel vulnerable.

Blue is the colour of the sky, reminding you that only the sky need be the limit. Blue is empowering in a different way from red, which is earthly empowerment. It signifies the potential for limitless spiritual development and is linked with Sahaqiel, Angel of the Sky, and Ascended Master El Morya.

PINK/GREEN. Apart from being associated with your heart chakra and the angel Haniel, the colour pink is for love and compassion. Green represents growth and renewal in your life and your connections to nature and the environment.

YELLOW/GOLD. Choose yellow to reinforce a wish for clarity and enlightenment. It represents sun energy and therefore the angel Raphael. Linked with your solar chakra, it focuses on joy, freedom from care and spontaneity.

ORANGE. Think orange for joyful vitality and activity. It symbolises artistic or other forms of creativity, and is also the colour of the angel Uriel's fire energy, which can cleanse and heal all the body's chakra centres (see the meditation on page 80).

RED. Ruby red, or crimson, is the colour for strong foundations and represents energy, power and the passion to succeed. It is also for forgiveness, enabling a new start to be made. Focus on the angel Camael with this colour, and the base chakra (see pages 25 and 26). Master Jesus is also associated with crimson (and with gold).

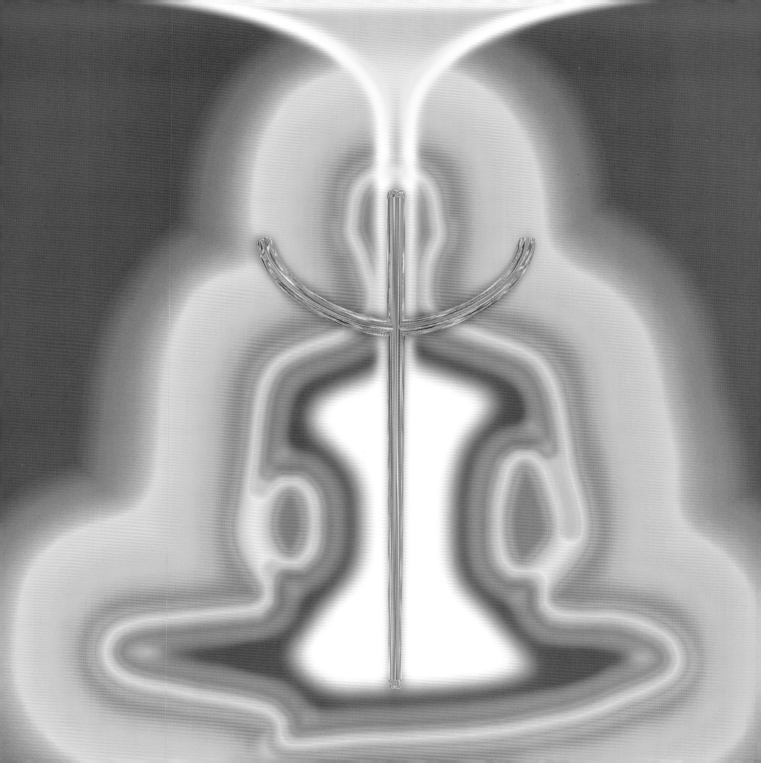

Strengthening and releasing meditation with Michael and his sword

First, decide whether you wish to release issues from within yourself, either of a physical nature, emotions you would like to overcome, or ties that bind you to another. Then consider what aspects of yourself you would like to strengthen or protect. See page 26 for general preparation for your meditation.

- Take some slow, deep breaths in and out and focus on your inner self.
- As you breathe inwards imagine you are breathing in pure white light.
- As you breathe outwards imagine you are breathing out anger, fear, worry or stress, and feel yourself relaxing and becoming calm.
- Feel tiny roots growing from your feet into the floor, grounding you.
- Open your energy chakras by visualising the flowers, starting with the red base chakra, then orange (sacral), yellow (solar), green (heart), sky blue (throat), indigo (brow or third eye) and violet (crown). See these flowers opening and focus on the colours in the areas of your body from which you want to either release or strengthen.
- Focus on your heart chakra and ask Michael to help you in Love and Light, Love and Light, Love and Light. See Michael in your mind, holding a sword of silvery metal.
- If you wish to sever a tie that binds you to another, ask from your heart.
- Next visualise your own first issue for release and focus on the chakra concerned. Imagine the sword cutting it away from within you. Feel it leaving your body, and disappearing in the golden light around you. Then take the next issue, and so on, and with each issue you release your body will feel lighter.
- When all the issues or ties have been released, ask Michael to fill you with strength and with blue healing energy.
- Now ask for any coloured healing rays that you need and feel them flowing into the chakra energy centres. Examine each chakra and see each flower glowing more brightly.
- Then close each one down to the bud as in previous meditations, asking Michael to seal and protect each of them in turn.
- Finally, ask Michael to wrap you in his blue cloak, for safety and security, and see yourself completely enveloped in cobalt blue. Thank him and the other angels for their help in this meditation. Take some deep breaths to bring yourself gently back to now, and open your eyes when ready.

Five light-hearted angel tips

You can call on help from angels not just for serious concerns but also for more mundane difficulties. Try these light-hearted tips when you are in need of an angel's helping hands in your everyday life.

- You are desperately trying to get to an important appointment and are running behind through no fault of your own. Ask Sadriel to change the traffic lights for you and Eth to create traffic order to speed up your journey.
- Following on from the above, ask Ambriel the problem-solving angel to ensure that a parking place is available for you – be sure to trust that it will be there.
- If you are behind with your work, ask Camael to give you the extra energy to make the whole process easier and faster.
- If there has been an argument in the room, ask Michael and his angelic crew to come in and vacuum up the negativity for you – with practice, you will be able to feel it disappear and lighter, cooler air take its place.
- If you have made time to do a meditation which is important to your well-being and don't want to switch off your phone line, ask Raphael to hold all phone calls and callers to the house unless vital.

- ANGELICA: MICHAEL'S HERB. The herb angelica (*Angelica archangelica*) has angelic significance, in particular the seeds and the stalk. The seeds are believed to represent the lightness of angelic realms, and the fragrance conjures up cosmic awareness and assistance from your guardian angel. The fragrance of the roots can draw angels closer and denotes a desire for spiritual expansion. The herb also represents Michael's sword, cutting through falsehood and revealing truth, allowing in the light to our deepest feelings. It can also bring compassion and understanding.

Zadkiel: *abundance, wisdom & success*

Zadkiel's name means 'Righteousness of God'. He is ruler of the planet Jupiter, sixth heaven, and chief of the order of dominions (see page 24). Amongst other things, he holds the key to wisdom and can help us to expand our horizons of possibility in all sorts of ways. One of these is in terms of career development, where he supports us with knowledge and memory, two most useful assets.

Zadkiel is the bringer of joyful abundance, tempered with responsibility and integrity. There are many kinds of abundance, including money, loving kindness, health, happiness and spirituality. Which do you seek, and why? Is the abundance you seek just for personal gain, or are you mindful of the effects of your actions on others? Remember the law of karma, which states that any good deeds we do, even if anonymous, will result in goodness coming our way, while actions of evil intent will rebound on us many times over. Zadkiel (who was the angel in the Bible who stopped Abraham's hand when he was about to sacrifice his son, Isaac) asks that we always use wisdom, thoughtfulness and mercy in our dealings with others.

A further responsibility of Zadkiel's is to help us to keep hold of our ideals. So often we have to accept compromise in order to maintain happy relationships, but if this is at the price of sacrificing our personal ideals, we are unlikely to achieve long-term happiness. Therefore, retain your idealism, even when it is easier to let go and opt for a quieter life. This may simply be a test of your inner resolve and strength of character.

In this chapter it is suggested that you consider what abundance you seek to make you successful in your own terms. You can then frame your personal affirmation to the Universe and send it using angel magic. When you receive your abundance, use it to help others. May Zadkiel's good luck find you.

Zadkiel's crystals are lapis lazuli and turquoise. Lapis lazuli, also called 'the eye of the gods', has been revered for thousands of years as representative of the mysterious starry heavens. It was believed to carry the means to acquire knowledge and magical powers. Turquoise is another ancient stone for courage, action and wisdom.

An angelic ritual for abundance and success

"In great humility, fill thy heart with the love of God, thou shalt then have a pure spirit which will grant (by the Lord's permission) thy desires. Therefore seek for that which is good; avoid all evil either in thought, word or action; pray to God to fill thee with wisdom, and then thou shalt reap an abundant harvest"
Trithemius' Book of Secrets – The Magus, Francis Barrett

Is your life so stressed that you can't see the wood for the trees? Is it all making you miserable? What kind of abundance will it take to make you happy? Ask the relevant angel to help you decide: Gabriel for hope, Raphael for health, Michael for strength and security, Cassiel for harmony and serenity, Camael for courage and self-empowerment, Haniel for love, Zadkiel for wisdom or success.

Now you need to become part of the flow of the Universe. In order to do this you could make a universal affirmation for the type of abundance you need, and ask Zadkiel for help to send this to the Universe. You can either use the affirmation below or compose your own to use in the ritual.

Carry out this ritual during a waxing moon, if possible three days before the full moon. You could perform the ritual in your home sanctuary or sacred space if you have created one (see pages 17 and 79), using your treasure box (see page 29).

You will need:
A deep blue or turquoise cloth; a candle to match; frankincense essential oil; a lapis lazuli or turquoise crystal; your prepared universal affirmation (if using your own version)

🖙 Take the candle, etch into it the sign for Jupiter and place it in the east (see illustration opposite for the symbol). Anoint your candle with a drop of frankincense oil to aid your quest.
🖙 Place your lapis lazuli or turquoise crystal in the west, which further secures your foundation, and aids wisdom and prosperity.
🖙 As you light the candle, call on the angel Zadkiel to assist you in the name of the planet Jupiter, and say that you wish to send your universal affirmation for your highest good.
🖙 Next read or recite your own or the following affirmation, from your heart, as follows:

"I am grounded and safe and with the help of the angels I open my heart to radiate love and light to the Universe. Earth, air, fire and water nourish me and give me life, wisdom and health. In return I send healing to Mother Earth, to her atmosphere and those within it, to her waters and those on or in them, to her soil and those who live by its bounty. I am part of the cosmos and the spark of the Divine is within me. The river of life flows through me; the abundance I need will come to me in surprising ways and obeying the universal laws I shall give as I mean to receive as an expression of my eternal gratitude to the Creator. As above so below, as below so above."

🕊 Now let your affirmation go. There is no need to dwell on it, simply send it and then forget about it.

🕊 If you can, leave your candle to burn out. If not, always snuff out candles, as you lose considerable energy (40%) by blowing them out.

🕊 You should start to experience your abundance within a few weeks of making the affirmation. Remember to give thanks to the angels at this time and thereafter.

🕊 WISHING ON A CRYSTAL FOR LUCK. You can use any crystal, although angelite, celestite or angelhair quartz are particularly appropriate. Choose a small crystal that will fit into the centre of your palm. Hold the crystal in your left palm, deciding in your mind on a suitable wish. Then invoke the angel of the day, say your wish three times over your chosen crystal adding the words: "In Love and Light, Love and Light, Love and Light". Finally, with your right palm push your wish into the crystal until your two hands are closed together. Your wish is then encapsulated, and you can carry your crystal around for luck.

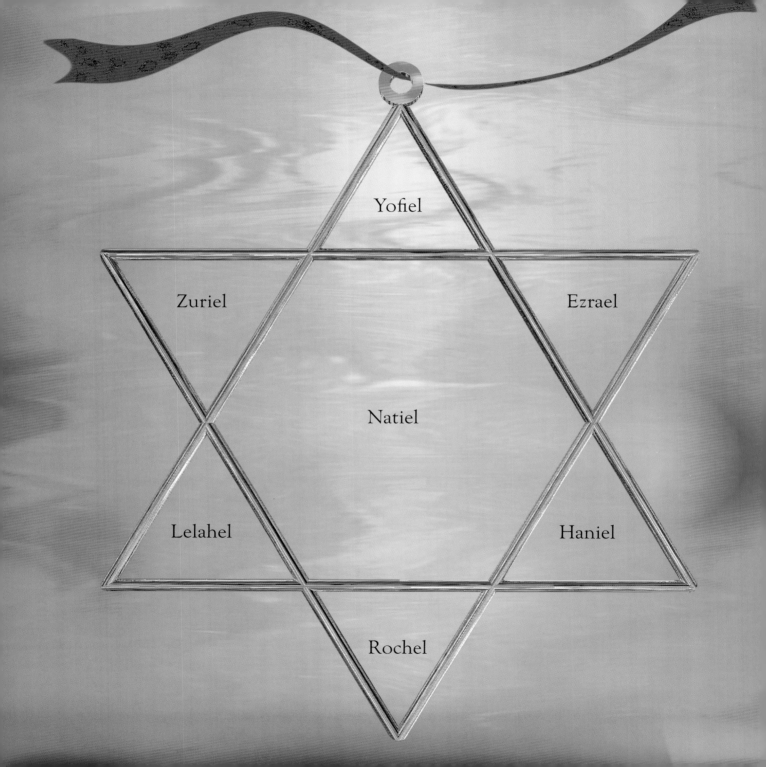

Lucky amulets and talismans

"For gaining much merchandising, they made a seal of silver, being the image of a man, sitting on a chair, holding a balance in his hand, and they perfumed it with well-smelling spices." Talismanic Magic, Francis Barrett

In days gone by, much was made of lucky talismans and amulets engraved with angels' names. Why not revive this custom, by selecting a name that seems right for you personally and either writing it on a piece of paper which you can keep in your pocket, or having it engraved on a medallion for a necklace or bracelet? You could use a crystal power bracelet, selecting either a crystal which corresponds to an angel who seems to have a personal appeal for you, or one linked to an appropriate chakra colour.

SOLOMON'S SEAL: THE SIX-POINTED STAR. Solomon's Seal, the six-pointed star shown in our illustration, is a very ancient and powerful symbol and is considered to represent the macrocosm, the whole Universe and the science of all things. Relatively recently it was adopted by the Jews and became their Star of David.

King Solomon is believed to have been an incarnation of the Ascended Master El Morya (see page 90) and was responsible for building his famous (and magical) temple in Jerusalem. He is supposed to have possessed *The Book of the Angel Raziel* (containing all the celestial secrets) and derived from it his knowledge of magic. This knowledge, together with a ring brought to him by Raphael, enabled him to command demons as slave labour to build the temple (rather like the genie of the lamp in the tale of Ali Baba).

If you combine your chosen angel with the seal of Solomon you will increase the power of the talisman. The angels in our illustration are for the following:

- Natiel: for dispelling negative energy.
- Yofiel: for bringing luck in exams, interviews or at work.
- Zuriel: for improving brain power.
- Ezrael: for courage.
- Lelahel: for love, art, science or fortune.
- Haniel: for loving relationships.
- Rochel: for finding something lost.

Meditation for wisdom and faith with Pistis Sophia, the earthly mother

This meditation invokes the angel Sophia, ancient symbol of faith and wisdom, the twelve stars above her head representing the Zodiac. Sophia has for centuries been equated with Eve, Isis, the Virgin Mary, and Kwan Yin (Ascended Lady Master and Divine Mother in Buddhism – 'She who hearkens to the cries of the world'). Sophia can guide you if you seek wisdom, she can comfort you and help you to triumph over adverse circumstances in order to find success and happiness.

Begin your meditation in the usual way (for basic information see page 26). For this exercise, remember that your left hand takes from the universal energy source and your right hand gives back; similarly your left foot takes and your right foot gives back energy.

- Place your hands palms upwards resting on your lap.
- Take some deep breaths to relax, detach and focus within, asking Zadkiel and Sophia to be with you.
- Open your seven chakra centres. Send roots from your feet into the floor to ground yourself.
- Now visualise golden light pouring into your crown chakra, and feel this love and light flowing down.
- The healing love and light will then radiate downwards to your feet.
- Send it through the roots in your feet into the earth.
- Now, through your heart chakra, become part of the infinity symbol, as pictured in our illustration of Sophia, symbol of the eternal mother, faith and wisdom.
- Start with your left foot and imagine drawing up blue earth energy through the base and sacral to your heart chakra, and then down to your right hand.
- Now imagine the twelve stars of Sophia extending from your right hand to your left hand, over your crown. Draw in golden star fire energy down your left arm, across and back to your heart chakra.
- Now send the energy down to your right foot and back into the earth, where it connects back with the deep blue energy and the crystal at the heart of the earth.
- You are now connected to the universal source by means of the infinity symbol.
- Invoke Sophia, embodiment of compassion and loving kindness. Ask her to help with the power of her sacred twelve stars for your highest good. Feel strength and guidance flow into you from the stars above and the earth below
- When you feel ready, return to now, seal each chakra, thanking the angels for their loving assistance.

Visible signs of spiritual growth

"An angel in a white robe, touching earth and heaven appeared. His wings were flame and a radiance of gold was about his head." The Symbolism of the Tarot, P.D.H. Ouspensky

THE RAINBOW-COLOURED AURA. Directly around our physical body, extending to about 3 cm, is a fairly thin layer known as the etheric sheath or physical auric body. The colour of this sheath varies according to our physical and spiritual wellbeing, and for those who can see auras it is immediately apparent if there is physical or other illness present. In most people it is light blue and becomes paler as you evolve spiritually.

The etheric auric body extends outwards from the etheric sheath and is three-dimensional. In those who are healthy, it comprises pure and clear rainbow colours in the same sequence as the chakras of the physical body, commencing with red nearest the body and ending with violet/magenta furthest away.

The energies of the aura and chakras are linked together to provide us with health. Poor health in an area of the body will result in a dimming of the chakra colour as well as the aura, which will be dark or jagged if people are very ill or abusing alcohol or hard drugs. Auras are affected by our emotions, becoming brighter when we are happy. Suppressed anger causes red flecks to appear. In people who are ill or not very grounded the auras are faint or dim, and it is said they disappear altogether in those close to death.

The colours within the etheric auric body are translucent and, to those who can see them, appear to shimmer as though alive. The size of the aura is not fixed and will fluctuate according to your activities. It will vary according to your interaction with others, expanding if you are with a friend and contracting if you are in less congenial company.

People who seek to grow spiritually and psychically gradually open up the spiritual chakras of crown, third eye and throat, so that these expand (the crown chakra expands upwards as a semi-circular curve). This in turn develops and refines the etheric sheath, which may become pure white.

🍂 AURAS OF ANIMALS, PLANTS AND CRYSTALS. While adult humans are the only beings to have rainbow-coloured auras (those around babies are pale blue or green), there are auras around all living things. Even an inanimate object has an aura that can be seen with practice. Crystals can be seen to give off a faint smoke emanating from the surface. Plants have a more yellowish aura while that around animals is usually blue or green.

🍂 SEEING OR SENSING AURAS. With practice, you can start to feel the auras around you; if you stretch your palms out fully and then gradually bring them toward your body you can feel the difference between the energies making up each layer. The energy further away feels stronger, while that close to the body feels softer and fluffier.

In time, you will also feel the energy around you change when you call in your angels, and if you hold out your hands palms outwards, you will sense their energy brushing your palms.

Again, with practice you would be able to see auras. Try it on yourself first. Darken the room, place your two hands in front of you (palms facing away), with the fingers pointing towards each other and just touching. If you then slowly draw them away from each other, you will see a faint radiance stretching in a line between them – like a sort of vapour trail. Keep practising and your ability will develop further.

🍂 HALOES: IMAGES OF THE WAY OF LOVE AND LIGHT. The white or gold haloes depicted in religious art, surrounding angels and the heads of holy figures, are representations of the light that emanates from within them. At the core of most belief systems is the search for the 'way of the light' and, once found, this light fills the individual's energy meridian and shows above the crown chakra, where white is the sum of all the seven chakra colours. This is sometimes represented as the 'thousand petalled lotus flower'. Angels are pure spirit and are often perceived as radiating white gold light; this is the light we picture when we ask for the light of the angels to surround, envelop and protect us during meditations or other exercises.

Seeking fame and fortune

"But else in deep of night, when drowsiness hath locked up mortal sense, then listen
To the celestial Sirens' harmony, that sit upon the nine infolded spheres,
And sing to those that hold the vital shears, and turn the adamantine spindle round
On which the fate of gods and men is wound." Arcades, John Milton

🕊 IN SEARCH OF ARTISTIC INSPIRATION. There are a number of special angels who have particular responsibilities in the creative world of the arts. For artists seeking inspiration from the soul, or for musicians who wish to give their finest performance, invocations may be directed to Israfel, Angel of Music; Hariel, Angel of Science and Arts; or Radueriel, Master of the Muses (art, poetry and music).

Remember that for creative inspiration to commence a project, you should invoke your chosen angels about three days away from the new moon (never at the time of the new moon itself, as the proportion of darkness to light is out of balance). To conclude an important project, invoke the angels at, or shortly before, the full moon.

For creativity out of doors, see also Cassiel (Chapter 7), which deals with harmony with the environment, including nature, the seasons, wildlife and the elements.

🕊 AT A CROSSROADS IN LIFE. Sometimes in life one is presented with a decision to make that involves taking some sort of chance or risk. Will is the ability to make the choice between different options. Invoke Tabris, Angel of Free Will, to help you choose for your highest good. Barakiel, as well as being Angel of Pisces and Scorpio, is the Angel for Games of Chance. He can be invoked to assist in bringing success if taking a gamble, but beware of being too greedy. If it is a question of gaining money, it is likely you will win only the amount of money you desperately need.

If worried about the future, you can ask Oriel, the Angel of Destiny, to give you the grace to accept whatever fate has in store for you.

Haniel: *love, compassion & beauty*

Haniel rules third heaven, the planet Venus (the star of love or evening star) and is one of the Angels of Creation. She is therefore primarily concerned with love, friendship, relationships and also sexuality. Chief of the angel order of virtues as well as principalities (see also page 24), in ancient times she was also associated with the Chaldean deity Ishtar. For millennia her name was engraved on good luck or love charms. She governs the month of December and the astrological sign Capricorn.

Love is the strongest force in the universe, encompassing loving partnerships, marriage, motherhood, friendship and even love for the earth itself. The principal duty of the angel order of virtues is that of working miracles on earth. These angels confer grace and bravery on deserving mankind, in accordance with how we treat and respect each other and our environment. In this context, our love should include compassion and sympathy for the less fortunate, and we can receive support from Haniel in connection with all these issues. However, first and foremost, you must be able to feel self-love, in the sense of being comfortable with yourself. We all have faults, and we must work to strengthen our good points and overcome our weaknesses.

Those whom we love, we love for the way they are, faults and all, and they feel the same about us. It doesn't matter whether you have a perfect face or physique – as long as your soul radiates love, you will be beautiful. Learn to follow the inner, still voice of your heart.

If you lack confidence or have low self-esteem, this chapter will help you. Man was not meant to undertake the journey of life alone; ask Haniel to guide you towards fruitful physical and spiritual companionship.

If you are shy in company and find it difficult to make friends, seek help from Haniel to help you overcome your shyness, Camael for strength and courage, and Michael to assist you to find the right words to start off a conversation. Then learn to become a good listener – in this way you will win many admirers.

Her crystals are rose quartz, emerald, jade or tourmaline. Pink crystals relate to love, friendships and affairs of the heart; green signifies personal development and growth.

Learning to love yourself

"It is only with the heart that one can see rightly; what is essential is invisible to the eye."
The Little Prince, Antoine de Saint-Exupery

Many people are constrained by what they think are other people's opinions of their appearance. They are afraid that if they don't conform to the world's standards of beauty and fashion, no one will love them. However, true beauty comes from within, from the spirit.

Learn to make the best of yourself and to emphasise your good points. Don't spend your life being envious of others' looks, because we must all grow old. Accept that neither you, nor the world, are perfect. Be kinder to yourself and accept your own faults, so that you can be more tolerant of the faults of others. When you are entirely happy with you, then you will be able to give love freely. Remember that the more positive you are about yourself, the more you can make things happen. Ask Haniel to surround you with love and fill you with warmth, and then enjoy sharing it with others.

Be brave! Changing how you look can bring more fun into your life, transforming your feelings about yourself and also the way people react to you. Try not to take yourself too seriously all the time and learn to laugh at yourself a little – it will do you good!

Dye your hair a bright colour one weekend and then step outside your door. The first step is the hardest. Once you have braved the stares of all those who wouldn't have the nerve to do it, they will admire your daring. Then you will feel the sense of liberation that goes with ceasing to care so much about what other people think. At that point you will have become your own person at last.

AN ANGEL STORY. A friend of mine worried continually about her daughter, who suffered with eating disorders. She received guidance through a dream as to the reason behind the problem. In her dream her daughter (an attractive girl) was in the company of an angel who showed her a mirror. The daughter saw in the mirror the reflection of an ugly person. "Who is this," she asked? "That is how you see yourself," replied the angel. "Now see how you really are," he said, and the reflection changed to her actual, attractive self. "When you are able to see how pretty you really are, and feel love for yourself, you will no longer have this disorder," advised the angel.

Loving and caring relationships

"The soul cannot live without love. All depends on providing it with a worthy object."
St Francis de Sales

🪶 LOVE AND PASSION. Angels are pure unselfish love and by their example they can help us to reinforce our own love for others.

Apart from Haniel, Angel of Love and Sexuality, guidance on the wisdom of a particular relationship may also be sought from the Shekinah. This great angel can be regarded as God himself in female form and was sometimes identified with the Holy Spirit. Legend says that she was first called down (from second heaven) by Abraham to live under the tree of life in the Garden of Eden. The Jewish people believe she can be invoked to bless your choice of partner.

If you need help in sexual matters, such as wishing to give maximum love and satisfaction to your partner, silently invoke Haniel at the appropriate moment, remembering to ask 'In Love and Light'. Similarly, for extra energy and passion you can call upon Camael.

In situations where jealousy has been aroused, ask Michael for either the strength to overcome it, or for his sword to cut away and release the bitterness. The Shekinah is also Angel of Liberation if, deep down, you know you need to move on.

🪶 ANGELS FOR CONCEPTION AND CHILDBIRTH. Perhaps you long for a family but feel so busy and stressed with daily life that you are having difficulty in making the right time and atmosphere to conceive. Use your home sanctuary (see page 17) to find peace and invoke assistance from Arduisher, Zoroastrian spirit for conception and childbirth. Also there is Yusamin, spirit of fertility, who is said to dwell in the 'wellsprings of light', or Samandriel, who will keep your prayer for conception until the time is exactly right. Pistis Sophia and Ascended Lady Master Kwan Yin can also help you (see pages 52 and 91).

According to *The Book of the Angel Raziel*, any of the following names can be worn, placed under the pillow or invoked for good luck during childbirth itself: Michael, Gabriel, Raphael, Haniel, Zadkiel, Uriel, Kidumiel and Rumiel. In addition, there is a special angel called Telemuch for the care and comfort of premature babies.

Remember always to ask for the support of the angels for your highest good. It may be that having a child is not for your highest good. If, sadly, this seems to be the case, ask Oriel, Angel of Destiny, to help you come to terms with the situation.

🪶 ANGELS FOR CHILDREN AND PET ANIMALS. Children from about four years upwards love to hear about angels, and most seem to have no difficulty in remembering some of the names. If you talk to your children about angels for the days of the week, teach them the name of the angel for the day on which they were born. Why not engrave this angel on to a medallion and place on to a crystal bracelet or necklace for them to wear when they are old enough? Both coral and amber are connected with babies and children and are considered very protective.

There are also angels specifically for pets, who can be invoked where appropriate (See also pages 76-7 for wild creatures). Tubiel is the angel for birds (and also for summer), while Hariel is responsible for tame animals. Manakel is the angel for aquatic animals, and Arariel is the angel for fish. If appropriate, hold the pet gently while doing your invocation. If you feel your pet needs some healing, ask the angels to help you give a little healing through your hands. For pets that are very ill, in pain or dying, ask the relevant angel to help release it with your love and compassion.

🪶 AN ANGEL STORY. A little seven-year-old boy I know called Joshua was with his mother at a Blue Angel card reading, and was allowed to select a card of his own from the pack. He could not see the faces of the cards, so that the selection was really being done by the angels, and the card he chose was the angel Camael, Angel of Justice, Empowerment and Courage (see Chapter 2). We discussed this selection and it transpired that he was being bullied at school. Camael wanted Joshua to know that he could call upon him to help deal with this situation. I found out later that Joshua now comes home and says to his mother "I called on Camael today to help me against the bullies and it definitely helps".

Cassiel: *peace, harmony & serenity*

Cassiel, 'Speed of God', is the angel of solitude and tears, ruler of seventh heaven, the order of cherabim, and the planet Saturn. Traditionally called the Angel of Temperance, he represents light and shade, or happiness and sadness, which if balanced lead to serenity. This means seeking to live as moderate and harmonious a life as possible.

Is your life tranquil and balanced, or are you completely overcome by stress or disorder? Perhaps you are coming to terms with overwhelming sadness. We all need time and space for contemplation, in order to identify and deal with the causes of our disharmony. Only by allowing this knowledge to come through can we take the inspired action that will convert challenge into opportunity and so rebalance life's light and shade. This chapter invites you to let go of disharmony and to achieve peace and serenity once again.

Some two thousand years ago the Essenes believed that in order to achieve wholeness within, it was necessary to harmonise the spiritual with the physical, and that the key to this was daily communion with angels. What greater desire can we have today than to try to achieve such harmony, not only within ourselves but also with our environment.

If you are dealing with bereavement, sorrow or rejection, you may feel at times that you are alone and surrounded by darkness. In fact, we are all part of the collective consciousness of nature. We mirror her perfection of form, which is in turn a galactic fragment of the Universe – itself, in the final analysis, a microcosm of the work of the Creator. By understanding and respecting nature and the earth, and by opting, with the help of the angels, to harmonise with them, you can regain your own equilibrium. Each of us holds a spark of the Divine, which some call our soul. If we open this up to love and light we can expand spiritually to become part of the cosmic web that is interwoven all around us, and by this means we need never feel alone.

Cassiel's crystals are obsidian, onyx, rutilated quartz and black agate. Obsidian is for seeing the shadow that also shows the light of hope. Onyx protects against enemies. Black agate is for courage.

Letting go of the past to find peace

"Looking backwards, we only remember the difficult periods of our lives, never the peaceful times; the latter are sleep, the former are struggle and therefore life." George Ivanovitch Gurdjieff

Most of us have some insecurities in our lives. How many of these were created years ago, when our parents or partners made us feel that our achievements or behaviour were never good enough?

Thought forms can be either positive or negative. As we have already seen, negative thought forms, if allowed to persist within our auras, will eventually lead to depression or even illness. Positive thought forms, on the other hand, can convert threats into opportunities, help us to set and achieve goals, and even to assist others more effectively. If you are at a very low point in your life, through bereavement or rejection, it may seem extremely hard to be positive at all. Seek help from the following angels.

Zagzagel: Angel of Wisdom, can give guidance on the best way for you to deal with a situation from the past. The Shekinah, Angel of Liberation, can support a need to be free to move on. Perhaps you have lost someone close to you, or need to give support to someone else in this position. Ask for loving help from Rachmiel, Angel of Mercy and Compassion, to help you to come to terms with the situation, let go of the person and be at peace. You can also send Rachmiel to help those you love who have been bereaved.

Try also either the visualisation for harmony (see page 74), or the meditation with the Angels of the Elements (see page 80), to help you to find your way forward to peace and serenity.

AN ANGEL STORY. A woman I know told me this tale of letting go of the past. In a meditation, she was aware of a very tall and splendid angel who was standing beside her, who took her hand to give comfort. "Why are you so much taller than me?" she asked. "Because of all the sorrows and hardships which you refuse to put behind you. They are stunting your growth," he replied. Taking this very much to heart, she asked for help in letting go of issues that had haunted her for years, and then endeavoured to put the suggestions into practice. In a later meditation she was suddenly aware of the same angel, but now she was nearly as tall as him. "You see," said the angel, "it is not that I am shorter but that you are taller, because you have worked to let go of your past and as a result you have grown and developed spiritually."

A visualisation for harmony: the circle of life and the cosmic web

"You are not enclosed within your bodies, nor confined to houses or fields,

That which is in you dwells above the mountain and roves with the wind,

It is not a thing that crawls into the sun for warmth or digs holes in darkness for safety

But a thing free, a spirit that envelops the earth and moves in the ether." The Prophet, Kahlil Gibran

If possible, do this visualisation in your indoor or outdoor sacred space (see pages 17 and 79).

- Take some deep breaths and feel yourself relaxing. Focus your attention within.
- Breathe in pure white light, and breathe out everything you wish to release from yourself.
- As you continue breathing deeply in and out, imagine you are filled with white light.
- Start to breathe out white light, and see it expand upwards and outwards until it is as if you are at the start of a pure white tunnel spiralling away from you. The angel Cassiel is with you as you travel along the white tunnel.
- You emerge from the tunnel into a beautiful place in nature. You are in a fragrant, sunny meadow full of wildlife, beside a clear stream which splashes over rocks and boulders.
- Suddenly your vision changes. You find that you can see the energy contained in everything around you. You are all translucent, formed of sparkling light. Instead of appearing solid, every single item and creature is made of millions of light particles scintillating in the sunshine.
- Now, filaments of light appear like gossamer, fine but strong, connecting you to everything you can see, and connecting everything to you. You are part of the collective consciousness of the Universal Source of life, comprised of love and light, uniting everything made by the Creator.
- Not only are you connected to everything on the earth, but also to the cosmic web itself. The angels Cassiel and Sahaqiel (Angel of the Sky) take your hands and you rise up into the sky. You become aware that the filaments of light join you, through the ether, to the solar system and stars. You are truly part of the Universe and you marvel at the revelation. You send love and light to the Universe and energy radiates back to you along the light filaments, completing the spiritual renewal of the circle of life.
- The angels return you gently to your white tunnel of air, reminding you that you can draw in the light to yourself and expel darkness by carrying out this exercise at any time. Thank the angels.
- Travel back along the tunnel, return your focus to now and open your eyes when ready.

A PRAYER TO THE ANGELS

*"Serapis Bey, Ascended Master and Angel, guide my thoughts
and my feelings skywards to heaven. Align me and bring me
in communion with the power of angels. Allow them to
enter into my life more fully, in order that I may acknowledge
and see their presence in everything which I do; in order that
I may feel them in every word which I speak; in order that
I may sense them in every emotion which I feel; in order that
I may experience them in my thoughts and in my life.*

*Draw close angels! Enter the circle of sacred space and join
me in my contemplation and meditation. Draw your soft
white wings around me, to protect me from the adversities
of life and keep me pure, clear and safe. Calm my worried
brow with your gentle hands; lay your tender kisses upon me;
soothe my mind and heart; free me from pain; enter into my
life, celestial beings of light, and bring your beauty and your
wonder, that I may see it and know it well."*

From the Chapter entitled *A Ritual for Connecting
with the Angels*, A Channelling from Serapis Bey,
from *The Ascended Masters' Book of Ritual and Prayer*,
Edwin Courtenay

Harmonising with nature and the elements

"Teach us sprite or bird what sweet thoughts are thine,
I have never heard praise of love or wine
That panted forth a flood of rapture so divine." Percy Bysshe Shelley

🪶 ANGELS FOR WILD CREATURES. Until very recently, man has felt superior to the animal kingdom, with much resulting cruelty. In the past, the idea that animals might have feelings would have been considered absurd, in fact a few hundred years ago even women were scarcely considered to have either brains or feelings. Fortunately, however, the majority of us now consider it important to respect the animal kingdom and to try to live in harmony with our environment. If you wish to help wildlife, either generally or in specific circumstances, you can invoke Thuriel, Angel of Wild Animals, Arael, Angel of Wild Birds, Arariel, Angel of Fish or Manakel, Angel of Aquatic Animals.

🪶 NATURE ANGELS. (These angels should not be confused with fairies, devas and elementals – who are different but nonetheless fascinating.)

Many of us find great comfort and tranquillity in being close to nature. This may take the form of walking in the countryside, sailing or being on water, or perhaps in cultivating a garden. There are many angels of nature that we can call upon, for instance Zuphlas, Angel of Forests. Trees provide us with vital oxygen and are important for the harmony and balance of the planet. Ask Zuphlas to nourish trees and cause them to grow strongly. Sachluph, Angel of Plants, can help wild flowers to grow. Sahaqiel is the Angel of the Sky, who can help the atmosphere as well as expanding your own personal horizons.

Each season of the year has special angels. Telvi is Angel of Spring, Casmaran, Angel of Summer, Andarcel is Angel of Autumn and Farlas, Angel of winter. Seek their help if you plan an outdoor project at a specific time.

For gardeners, there is Shamshiel. Associated with both Paradise and the Garden of Eden, this great angel can be invoked if you are about to design or renovate a garden and wish to create something of lasting beauty.

Sachluph will help you to achieve strong and healthy flowers or shrubs, while Sofiel is Angel of Vegetables and Fruit. Matriel, Angel of Rain, can bring relief and healing through the element of water, as can Ariel. If you have a plant that is sickly, hold it gently and ask Ariel to send healing to the plant through the energy of earth, air or water.

Creating a sacred space outdoors ❧

Perhaps you have created a sacred space or sanctuary within your home (as suggested on page 17). Why not consider a similar area outdoors in your garden, designed around an angel of your choice. It will take about 20 minutes, so try to ensure you will not be disturbed during this time.

❧ THE ELEMENTS. For all types of healing you should try to represent the four elements of earth, air, fire and water, plus, if you feel it is appropriate, stone and metal. Earth and air are already in residence, so to speak. You could incorporate a water feature (some are self-contained and made of stone or earthenware, and some are made of rock crystals). If you don't feel comfortable about real fire, you can either use a sculpture or mobile representing fire in some way, or a crystal such as clear quartz or amber which symbolise fire or the sun. For the latter, this should be placed in such a way that you can create a circle around it (sacred symbol of the sun), either in the soil or by raking concentric circles in gravel. If there is space, create an archway of metal or stone in which to frame a seat, where you can relax or meditate.

❧ CHOOSING AN ANGEL. Next, choose one of our seven main angels – the one which seems to embody your life needs. You can then include a special shape for your chosen angel, for instance the caduceus (symbol of healing) for Raphael, or a planetary symbol. You could use one of these shapes to create a flowerbed, or alternatively you could engrave the symbol on to a wall or make it up in metal or plastic and suspend it from a tree.

❧ THE PLANTING. Specific flowers can be planted both to help with the invocation of your chosen angel, and also to bring angels closer in general. For instance, hyacinths in the spring, followed by jasmine in the summer, are 'calling flowers' for angels. Herbs also have significance – sage, for instance, is cleansing, and thyme gives strength and courage. Then, if you have chosen the angel Zadkiel, you would select deep blue and blue-purple flowers, such as pansies, irises and anemones. With the angel Haniel you would plant pink roses and honeysuckle, and if you create a pond you could plant pink waterlilies. There is much else that can be done to create a sacred outdoor space with special angelic significance. For other ideas or assistance see Further Reading on page 96.

Meditation with the angels of the elements for inner healing and harmony

"Be still and know that I am God." Essene Prayer

For basic meditation instructions, see page 26.

🐦 Breathe deeply, open your chakra energy centres and ground yourself with roots into the floor.

🐦 Focus within and see yourself on top of a high hill, gazing down on beautiful countryside. The air is clear and cool; breathe deeply of its purity. As you gaze at the panoramic views, the scene brings tears to your eyes. Let them flow – this alone will give you a sense of release.

🐦 Suddenly a dove flutters in front of you and hovers over a pathway down the hillside. You walk along the path, which winds downwards towards a valley. You become aware of the sound of water and, as you turn a corner, you see a stream in front of you, which tumbles down the hill and becomes a small waterfall.

🐦 You come upon a cave behind the waterfall, carved out of white marble. Beside it you see the angel Cassiel. He is dedicated to your inner peace and harmony and invites you to enter the cave. As you step into the cave a dazzling light fills you, highlighting the areas for healing.

🐦 You then see Phul, Angel of Water. He asks you to stand under the waterfall spray. As this spray washes over you, feel the negativity clouding your emotions being washed away, leaving you soothed, cleansed and reborn.

🐦 You move into the cave itself. In front of you stands Uriel, angel of fire, holding a burning candle. You ask Uriel to surround you with the sacred fire of the candle. Feel the flame entering your crown and gradually passing through each chakra, clearing blockages, purifying, and healing old issues that are preventing your physical and spiritual wholeness. The energy travels down and exits from your root chakra, enabling you to feel lighter of body and spirit.

🐦 Now the angel Ariel appears. Ask Ariel to help you to draw in earth energy to cauterise and heal the space created by the cleansing and purifying process. Feel a wave of blue-purple energy travelling up from your feet through each energy chakra until it reaches your crown. Then draw in golden energy from your crown right down to your toes, to seal in the healing. Thank the elemental angels and return to Cassiel. Now, as you stand in the pure white light, there is no shadow within you – you are a child of the light.

🐦 Slowly return to normal consciousness. Remember to close your chakras, ensuring they are sealed and protected and thank all the angels who assisted.

Raphael: *healing, energy & knowledge*

Raphael's name means 'God has Healed'; he rules the sun, second heaven and the west wind. Of Chaldean origin, he is guardian of the tree of life and knowledge in the Garden of Eden and, since ancient times, has been charged with the healing of the earth. Sacred texts recorded that through him the earth is made a suitable dwelling place for man, whom he also heals of all maladies. Legend states that after the Flood it was he who gave a book of science and knowledge (*The Book of the Angel Raziel*) to Noah to rebuild the world.

We are all made up of energy and are born with the capacity either to embrace the world (be positive) or turn our back on it (allowing negativity to dominate). If we are ill, doctors prescribe drugs to alleviate the symptoms, but our problems may be more deeply rooted. In breathing and eating, we absorb energy in and out of our physical body; this exchange ceases only with death. However, what we are taking in, and how we are doing it, is equally important. Many people breathe too shallowly, depriving themselves of sufficient energy; others have a poor diet that lacks vitamins and minerals. Stress affects our physical and mental wellbeing. All these factors deplete the body chakras and therefore health. The good news is that angels can help us to release this negativity if we will let them.

As patron angel of healing, Raphael is the most important angel who can be invoked in this connection. We can also ask Raphael to help us heal the earth, including the atmosphere, the seas, and the animal and mineral kingdoms. It is said that healing is the gift of spirit and comes from the universal source, which is comprised of love and light, the two most powerful forces in the cosmos. We are all surrounded with this energy. Spiritual healers act as channels to direct it into themselves and others, but in fact anyone is capable of accessing a little energy, given sufficient focus and the right frame of mind. The rays can be absorbed to strengthen your energy chakras and immune system, thus facilitating the body's ability to self-heal. Try the exercises in this chapter and commence the process towards health and wholeness.

Raphael's crystals are diamond or clear quartz, to give energy at all levels and develop hidden talents.

Raphael's golden ball of healing energy

"I am the angel of the sun,
Whose flaming wheels begin to run,
When God's almighty breath
Said to the darkness and the night,
Let there be light! And there was light
I bring the gift of faith" The Golden Legend – Raphael, Henry Wadsworth Longfellow

If you have tried our meditation, you will have understood how healing can be channelled into the energy centres of your body. Now you can try to send some healing to others. You may not be as proficient as spiritual healers themselves, who receive special training, but you can certainly help those in need.

- Sit quietly in a chair and focus your mind within yourself.
- Take some deep, relaxing breaths and ask Raphael to surround you with the golden healing energy of the sun.
- Open up the energy meridian within you, that is, open all the chakra centres.
- Feel a golden energy ball (about the size of a tennis ball) entering your crown and imagine it travelling down through the spiritual chakras. Focus on the fact that you are asking for this energy to give healing and love to someone.
- As the energy ball reaches your heart, expand it with love so that it is the size of a football. Feel it travel down, gathering energy, until it reaches your base chakra.
- Now imagine it exiting from your base chakra and catch it between your two palms. You will actually feel the energy ball within your hands.
- Ask Raphael to help you send this energy to the person who needs it, and ask that the person's own guardian angel helps them to receive the healing for their highest good.
- Say that you wish to send the healing to (person's name) 'in Love and Light, Love and Light, Love and Light'. As you say the words, slowly and very gradually close your hands together, and visualise the healing going to the nominated person. Try to end your invocation at the point where your palms close together. You will find you placed your hands in the prayer position. Thank your angels.

A journey into an aquamarine crystal:
a blue-green visualisation for emotional healing

🐦 Begin by sitting comfortably and, if possible, holding an aquamarine (or other blue-green) crystal in your left hand. Breathe deeply until you reach the point at which you are relaxed and calm. Visualise protective golden light all around you, and roots anchoring your feet to the floor and therefore grounding you.

🐦 Now invoke Phul, a powerful angel who is Lord of all the Waters and Powers of the Moon. The power of the moon controls the tides and influences our moods. Phul is associated with the crystal aquamarine, stone of the emotions. Aquamarine, meaning 'water of the sea', is also a talisman for journeys over water.

🐦 Take the hand of the angel and imagine that you are becoming very small and going into the aquamarine or similar crystal that you hold; you are completely surrounded by the colour aquamarine. Suddenly your vision clears and you are standing beside a turquoise sea. The sky is an aquamarine dome above you. The sun is shining, the water is very clear. The waves gently lap the shore, with the surf creaming on to the sand.

🐦 Suddenly you see dolphins swimming towards you. You count them – one to seven – and, as you count each dolphin, you feel more and more peaceful and relaxed. They seem to want you to join them and you sense their love and protection. You wade a little way into the sea, so that the dolphins can form a circle around you and focus aquamarine energy towards you.

🐦 You now ask Phul to help you receive the emotional healing that is being offered, and you feel the soothing and healing crystalline energy flowing over and around you together with the ripples of the sea. Allow the pure blue-green to wash through you, dissolving away anger, fear, sorrow or despair. Use this energy to listen to your inner voice and to decide how you really wish to feel in future and how to deal with the situation which caused your emotional strife or entanglement. Having washed away the negative emotions, you will feel reborn and lighter of spirit. Thank the dolphins for their care and concern and return to the shore, counting the dolphins from seven back to one as you do so.

Finally, ask Phul and Raphael to seal in the healing you received, and then gently return to normal consciousness. Open your eyes when ready and thank the angels for their loving assistance.

Achieving positive health and well-being

"Angels are not the destination, but the route to it. Nor do they travel our journey for us, only assist us on our way"
The Fragrant Heavens, Valerie Ann Worwood

Now we have reached the twenty-first century, people are more conscious than ever before about good nutrition and a healthy lifestyle. As well as healing, Raphael is the Angel of Science and Knowledge, and he can be invoked to support you in finding the key to your own personal well-being. In addition, if you are striving to improve your general fitness, there are a number of other angels who may be able to assist.

🖎 LIFE, AGEING AND GENERAL WELL-BEING.

🖎 If you seek a long life, Rehael is Angel of Longevity. You might ask this angel for support either for yourself or for someone you love.

🖎 Another angel for assistance in health matters is Hamaliel, who can give some support in general health issues for yourself and your family.

🖎 The angel Muriel can be invoked for help with your concerns over ageing. You can ask Muriel to help you to increase the flow of energy through your body and to help you direct it to your key glands and organs, and that you receive maximum benefit from the air that you breathe and the food you eat.

🖎 The angel Uriel assists Raphael in healing mankind, and is the Angel of Fire. Apart from specific healing contained within the element of fire itself, Uriel can bring about transformation within oneself.

🖎 Phul, Lord of the Waters, is the angel who can particularly help with healing of emotional issues.

🖎 Ariel, one of the Rulers of Air (as well as Earth) can assist with bodily issues involving air, such as breathing, tiredness, respiratory viruses and general lack of energy. Use smoky quartz crystals also to absorb negative energy. (For a healing visualisation with Phul, see page 87, and for a meditation with all three angels see page 80.)

🖎 If you feel that your health is being affected by a possible deficiency in your diet (or food allergy), consult Isda, Angel of Food and Nourishment to mankind. If interpreted as physical nourishment, you could invoke Isda to help you to find out where the deficiency lies. One way of checking this is by dowsing over certain foods and asking for guidance (see page 21: Dowsing with a crystal). Isda can also be invoked to help deal with cravings for food if you are trying to reduce weight; also ask her to help you reduce your appetite or speak to her whenever you feel tempted.

🕊 You could also seek help from Achaiah, who deals with patience and the secrets of nature, both of which may be helpful in your quest. If you are exploring complementary medicine and/or homeopathic remedies, mentally ask Achaiah to guide your choice.

🕊 SENDING GIFTS OF ANGEL ENERGIES TO THOSE IN NEED. Now that you understand the principle of sending a golden ball of healing to someone (see page 84), you can use this in other ways also. Here are four other ideas:

🕊 Invoke a deep rose-pink energy ball of love with angel Haniel and send it to someone who needs love in their life.

🕊 Ask for a deep blue energy ball with angel Zadkiel, and send abundance to someone.

🕊 With angel Michael, either ask for emerald green (for growth) or cobalt-blue to send protection.

🕊 Invoke a crimson ball with Camael to send someone energy and strength.

🕊 AN ANGEL STORY. About a year ago I carried out a healing (I am a Reiki Seichem teacher and healer) on a lady named Heather, who is an extremely gifted psychic. At the start of the healing, in accordance with my usual practice, I silently invoked the protection of Ascended Master St Germain and the Silver Violet Flame Angels, and a little later I asked for Raphael to assist me with the healing. One can feel the healing energy increase when the angels are called in.

Afterwards, I asked Heather how she had found the experience. "Very powerful," she replied. She said that she had seen many colours, and with regard to the elements, she was particularly aware of the healing power of water, having seen herself in the sea with dolphins around her, which was appropriate to her need for emotional healing. She actually felt as if water was trickling over her. She told me that at one point early on in the healing an angel had stepped forward to add to the healing. This proved to be at the moment when I had called upon Raphael to help. She also saw a rainbow angel helping me with the healing; this was interesting because Seichem healing involves channelling rainbow colours which flow through the healer's hands. (I was told recently that this would have been Melchisadec, one of whose symbols is the rainbow.)

Angel healing with fragrances and oils

The knowledge of healing with elemental energy dates back thousands of years. Archaeologists believe that both crystals and oils were used to enhance healing in Ancient Egypt. This knowledge is now being rediscovered.

ANGELS AND THE ASCENDED MASTERS. The Ascended Masters are perfected souls who were once like us, but who have completed many incarnations, released all karma, and no longer need to live upon the earth. Together with angels, they are very close to God and give help and guidance to those who are willing to receive their assistance.

Each of these Masters works closely with angels, using the vibrational energies of the colour rays with which they are associated to guide you on particular life issues, and to help you to strive towards unconditional love.

The following three Ascended Masters work specifically with some of the angels mentioned in this book and may also be invoked in rituals with these angels. Colour and crystal essences may be purchased to further enhance the energies experienced.

SERAPIS BEY (see page 75) is linked with the angel Seraphiel. Colour ray – pure white/starfire. Helps to heal karma and to balance and harmonise you in life between happiness and sadness, expanding your potential and bringing you closer to angels generally with the power of love, joy, wonder and wisdom.

ST GERMAIN (see page 33) is linked with the angel Melchisadec. Colour ray – silver/violet. Guardian of the Silver Violet Fire and the Angels of the Violet Flame. Helps by bringing you the opportunity for spiritual alchemy, to strengthen your connections with God and the angelic spheres, and to transmute all negative, dark energy within or around you back to positive, white light.

LADY KWAN YIN (see page 52) is linked with Pistis Sophia, the Heavenly Mother. Colour ray – orange/pink. Helps with developing pure love and compassion for the sorrows of the world, and brings healing energy coupled with a feeling of unity with God, the angels, the Universe and all Creation.

CALLING ANGELS WITH FRAGRANCES. Fragrances have vibrational effects in the same way as crystals, and some are believed to 'call' angels to us. We cannot be sure how this works; it may be that these fragrances are close to those in the angelic realm itself, or perhaps using a particular scent makes our need for communication clearer to the angels. Carnation, frankincense, narcissus, hyacinth and rose are all general fragrances that will 'call' angels. Either burn a perfumed candle, or use them in an oil burner, before communicating or meditating with your chosen angel. Over and above this, in the same way as you feel drawn to certain crystals, you may also be attracted to fragrances which are right for you.

USING OILS FOR HEALING. You can add a further dimension to chakra healing by using fragrances/essential oils for each chakra. Here are some examples, although there are many more available:

Base	*Bodily strength, self-belief, survival, forgiveness.*	
	Patchouli or Rosewood. Thyme for courage (do not use when pregnant).	
Sacral	*Sexuality, creativity, sensuality, intimacy.*	
	Sandalwood or Benzoin. Pine for creativity.	
Solar	*Accomplishments, control and self-image.*	
	Ylang Ylang or Lime. Ginger for stimulation to action.	
Heart	*Love, compassion, surrender, acceptance.*	
	Jasmine or Rose.	
Throat	*Speaking/hearing the truth, spontaneity.*	
	Chamomile or Cypress.	
Third Eye	*Wisdom, discernment, spiritual vision.*	
	Hyacinth, cedarwood. Rosemary (do not use when pregnant).	
	Nutmeg for transmuting old thought patterns.	
Crown	*Cosmic awareness, consciousness of Love and Light force.*	
	Frankincense, rose, or lavender. Neroli for spiritual growth.	

The place of rainbows meditation

This powerful final meditation will enable you to harmonise yourself spiritually and physically, by receiving healing in both your aura and all the chakra energy centres of your body, engendering peace and relaxation and increasing your overall sense of health, harmony and well-being. For basic meditation instructions, see page 26.

- Take some deep breaths to relax, detach and focus within, invoking Raphael to be with you and growing roots into the floor to ground yourself.
- Open up the energy chakras, visualising their colours.
- Draw energy from the Universal Source through each chakra, feeling it travelling down to your toes. Send it through roots in your feet into the earth. See the earthly globe in your mind and imagine the healing rippling right around it.
- Now imagine yourself standing high on a sacred mound. You marvel at the breathtaking scenery – the work of the Creator. The air is cool and invigorating; breathe deeply of it.
- Below you is a grove of trees. You walk down the side of the mound until you reach the blue shade of the trees and, as you enter the shade, you immediately become part of the stillness and quiet atmosphere. Emerging from the trees, you feel the warm sun on your face. In front of you is a huge crystal pyramid and, as the sun strikes it, glorious rainbows are formed.
- The angels Raphael, Ariel and Melchisadec are waiting beside the pyramid. They beckon you forward and presently you stand in front of the pyramid itself. A door in the pyramid slides open, allowing you to enter.
- In the centre of the pyramid is the eternal flame, which is pale blue. As you stand in front of this flame, stretch out your hands and ask for earth, sky and rainbow healing, for your highest good.
- Ariel brings blue-purple energy from the earth into your base chakra, golden energy flows from Raphael and the sun into your crown. Then Melchisadec sends rainbow colours to fill the pyramid, flowing over and through you. Feel the appropriate colour ray enter each chakra, until all seven glow with dazzling light energy. Now imagine the colours radiating outwards into your aura and visualise it sparkling. Feel recharged with health and vitality.
- Ask the angels to bring you back to your physical body. Examine the chakras, which should be brighter in colour with more balanced energy outputs.
- Breathe deeply three times to ground yourself and return to normal consciousness.
- When you are ready, close each chakra, and don't forget to send love and light to Raphael, Ariel and Melchisadec for their help.

A-Z of Angels

Throughout the book we have suggested angels who can help in particular situations, but there are inevitably many that we have been unable to cover. Here we hope you will find angels to whom you can turn for help:

Adaptability - *Ambriel*

Air - *Casmaron* or *Ariel*

Anger (righteous) - *Camael*

Animals (tame) - *Hariel*

Animals (wild) - *Thuriel*

Arts - *Radueriel*

Assertiveness - *Machidiel*

Autumn - *Torquaret*

Benevolence - *Zadkiel*

Birds (tame) - *Tubiel*

Birds (wild) - *Arael*

Bravery/courage - *Verchiel* or *Camael*

Chance - *Barakiel*

Communication - *Michael* or *Ambriel*

Compassion - *Rachmiel*

Conception - *Lailah*

Daylight - *Shamshiel*

Deeps (Sea or Water) - *Rahab*

Deliverance - *Pedael*

Destiny - *Oriel*

Divination of the Future - *Eistibus*

Dreams - *Gabriel*

Earth - *Ariel* or *Michael*

Fertility - *Yusamin*

Fire - *Uriel* or *Nathaniel*

Fish - *Arariel* or *Rahab*

Food (physical and spiritual) - *Isda*

Forests/trees - *Zuphlas*

Forgetfulness - *Purah*

Fortitude - *Camael*

Freewill - *Tabris*

Friendship - *Mihr*

Fruit/Fruit Trees/Vegetables - *Sofiel*

Future - *Isiaiel*

Healing/Health - *Raphael* or *Hamaliel*

Heroism - *Narsinha*

Hope - *Phanuel* or *Gabriel*

Imagination - *Barakiel*

Impulsiveness - *Machidiel*

Individuality - *Machidiel*

Intuition - *Barakiel*

Joy - *Raphael* or *Gabriel*

Judgement and Justice - *Zadkiel*

Knowledge - *Zadkiel*, *Raphael* or *Raziel*

Light - *Gabriel* or *Mihr*

Lightning - *Barakiel*

Lost objects - *Rochel*

Love - *Haniel* or *Rahmiel*

Loyalty - *Verchiel*

Luck - *Yofiel*

Memory - *Zadkiel*

Mercy - *Rachmiel*

Mountains - *Rampel*

Music - *Israfel*

Mysteries - *Raziel*

North - *Uriel*

Optimism - *Adnachiel*

Order/tidiness - *Sadriel*

Patience/calmness - *Achaiah* or *Tual*

Peace - *Michael*, *Raphael*, *Gabriel* or *Phanuel*

Poetry - *Israfel* or *Vretil*

Prayer - *Metatron*

Problem-solving - *Michael* or *Ambriel*

Psychic development - *Barakiel* or *Ariel*

Rain - *Matriel*

Repentance - *Phanuel* or *Michael*

Salvation - *Haurvatat*

Secretiveness - *Muriel*

Security - *Tual*

Self-belief - *Machidiel*

Sky - *Sahaqiel*

Sleep - *Michael*

Solitude - *Cassiel*

South - *Raphael*

Spring - *Spugliguel*

Strength - *Michael* or *Zeruch*

Tears - *Cassiel* or *Sandalphon*

Time - *Eth*

Versatility - *Ambriel*

Vision (power of) - *Adnachiel*

Voyages - *Susubo*

Vulnerability/sensitivity - *Muriel*

Water - *Phul*

West - *Gabriel*

Winter - *Amabael*

Wisdom - *Zagzagel*, *Pistis Sophia*, *Metatron*

Womb - *Armisael*

Work relationships - *Hamaliel*